ARE YOU READY TO TAKE ON THE ACTIVITIES?

A BOOK BY

PARLOUR ROYCE PUBLICATIONS

2022

CONTENTS

TOP SQUAD: FRANCE 2018

TAKE A LOOK AT THIS FAMOUS WORLD CUP WINNING SQUAD.
GIVE IT A RATING ONCE YOU HAVE TAKEN A GOOD LOOK!

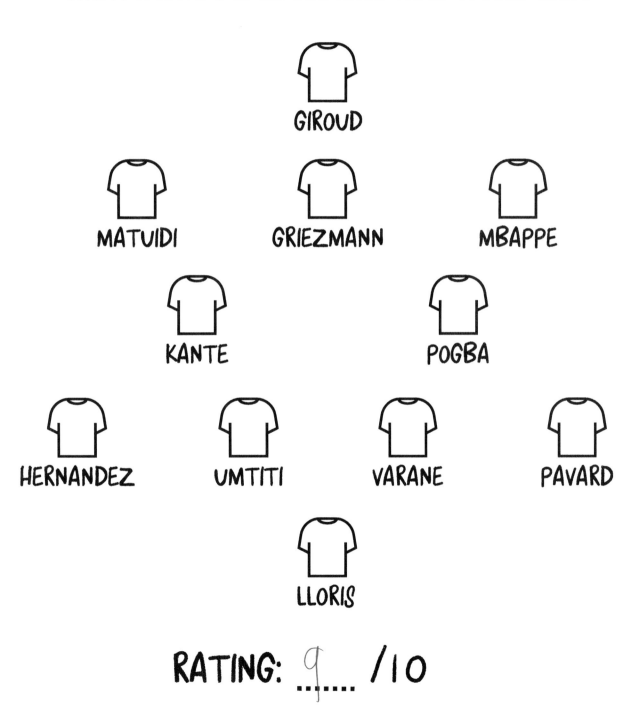

GIROUD

MATUIDI GRIEZMANN MBAPPE

KANTE POGBA

HERNANDEZ UMTITI VARANE PAVARD

LLORIS

RATING: 9 /10

ORDER UP OPERATION

CAN YOU ORDER THESE PAST PLAYERS FROM HIGHEST TO LOWEST IN TERMS OF WORLD CUP GOALS?
1ST = MOST GOALS, 4TH = LEAST GOALS

KLOSE

MARADONA

ROONEY

ROBBEN

1ST ....

2ND ....

3RD ....

4TH ....

ANSWERS ON PAGE 77!

MATCH UP MISSION

DRAW A LINE TO MATCH UP THE TEAM TO THEIR USUAL HOME KIT COLOURS

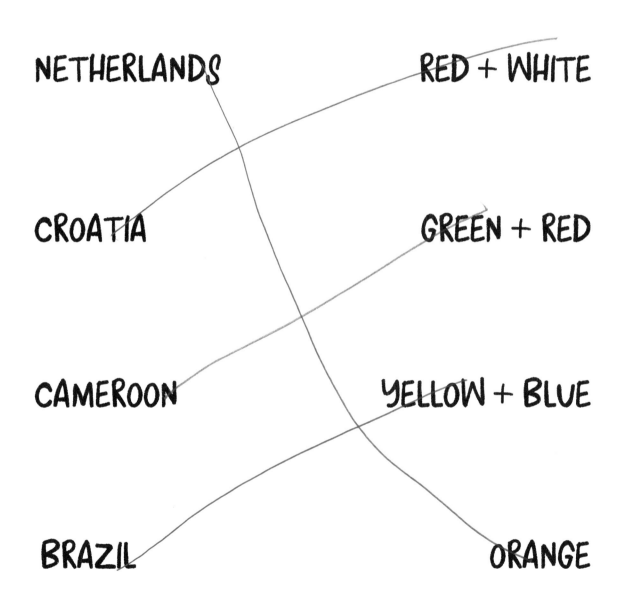

NETHERLANDS   RED + WHITE

CROATIA   GREEN + RED

CAMEROON   YELLOW + BLUE

BRAZIL   ORANGE

ANSWERS ON PAGE 61!

WORLD CUP FACTS: MOMENTS

TAKE A LOOK AT THESE FACTS RELATING TO SOME OF THE BEST MOMENTS FROM THE WORLD CUP

- ⚽ DIEGO MARADONA'S FAMOUS 'HAND OF GOD' GOAL WAS SCORED DURING THE QUARTER FINAL MATCH OF THE 1986 WORLD CUP BETWEEN ARGENTINA AND ENGLAND. ARGENTINA THEN WENT ON TO WIN THE TOURNAMENT

- ⚽ IN EXTRA TIME OF THE 2006 WORLD CUP FINAL, ZINEDINE ZIDANE GOT SENT OFF, LEAVING FRANCE WITH 10 MEN WHEN HE HEAD-BUTTED AN ITALIAN PLAYER. ITALY THEN WENT ON TO WIN THE FINAL

- ⚽ IN 1950, A RECORD WAS SET FOR THE HIGHEST ATTENDANCE AT A FOOTBALL MATCH. ALMOST 200,000 FANS WATCHED BRAZIL VS URUGUAY AT THE MARACANA STADIUM

ANAGRAMS: PLAYERS

REARRANGE THE LETTERS TO WORK OUT WHAT PLAYER IS MADE UP OF THE SCRAMBLED WORD

RZAHDA = ...

EABL = ...

LARAPMD = ...

LUPOY = ...

ANSWERS ON PAGE 80!

KIT DESIGN

HAVE A GO AT DESIGNING YOUR ULTIMATE WORLD CUP FOOTBALL KIT!

QUIZ: TEAMS

CAN YOU ANSWER ALL OF THE QUESTIONS BELOW CORRECTLY?

1) WHICH TEAM WON THE FIRST EVER WORLD CUP? *Uruguay*

2) HOW MANY TIMES HAVE URUGUAY WON THE WORLD CUP? *2*

3) WHAT TEAM IS NICKNAMED 'THE THREE LIONS'? *England*

4) WHAT ARE THE USUAL COLOURS OF AREGNTINA S HOME JERSEY? *blue and white*

5) WHAT YEAR DID ENGLAND FIRST HOST THE WORLD CUP? *1966*

ANSWERS ON PAGE 84!

WORD SEARCH: TOP MANAGERS

CAN YOU FIND ALL THE WORLD CUP MANAGERS IN THE WORD SEARCH?

```
T B S U K A O R C P S A C M B
S M A R T I N E Z Q O K U A I
C R A C D R R G Q L U E J N L
A A H E E O L D S T T A A C A
R M O O L R I A S S H Y C I V
V S T A B E Q J N W G E K N W
E E C S O E L O B T A R S I J
S Y P E S B F Y K I T O O T R
R A N N Q C G T N N E I M C E
W C N O U D E S C H A M P S C
X J R T E Y I S O J R A Q N E
U N G W O F D R E W K L O W N
V T X H U S X D A L I C H E N
```

DESCHAMPS	MANCINI	RAMSEY
DEL BOSQUE	MARTINEZ	LOW
SOUTHGATE	SANTOS	DALIC

ANSWERS ON PAGE 89!

8

WHO AM I? #1

USE THE CLUES TO WORK OUT THE MYSTERY WORLD CUP PLAYER

1)   I CAPTAINED MY NATIONAL TEAM

2)   I USUALLY WORE THE NUMBER 7 SHIRT

3)   I INSPIRED THE FILM 'BEND IT LIKE ...'

Beckham
....

ANSWER ON PAGE 67!

MATCH UP MISSION

DRAW A LINE TO MATCH UP THE WORLD CUP STADIUM TO ITS LOCATION

MARACANA STADIUM   SOUTH AFRICA

WEMBLEY STADIUM   MEXICO

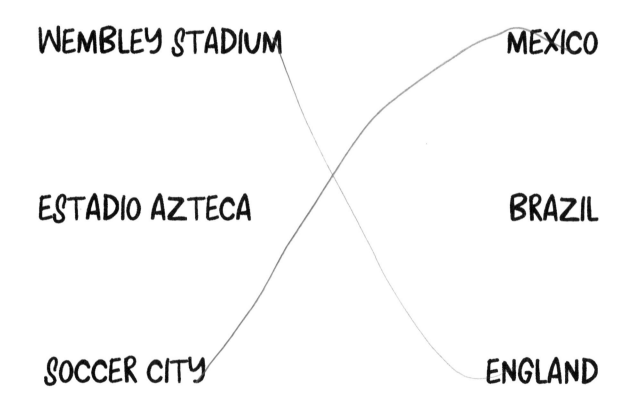

ESTADIO AZTECA   BRAZIL

SOCCER CITY   ENGLAND

ANSWERS ON PAGE 62!

WORLD CUP FACTS: WINNERS

TAKE A LOOK AT ALL OF THE TEAMS WHO HAVE WON WORLD CUPS IN THE PAST. THIS INFORMATION IS CORRECT UP UNTIL THE 2022 WORLD CUP!

TEAM	TITLES WON
BRAZIL	5
GERMANY	4
ITALY	4
ARGENTINA	2
FRANCE	2
URUGUAY	2
ENGLAND	1
SPAIN	1

ORDER UP OPERATION

CAN YOU ORDER THESE PAST PLAYERS FROM HIGHEST
TO LOWEST IN TERMS OF WORLD CUP CAPS?
1ST = MOST CAPS, 4TH = LEAST CAPS

LAHM   THIERY HENRY

GERRARD   PELE

1ST ....

2ND ....

3RD ....

4TH ....

ANSWERS ON PAGE 76!

MANAGER CHALLENGE

YOU HAVE A MAXIMUM OF £100 MILLION TO SPEND ON YOUR ULTIMATE WORLD CUP TEAM. OVER THE NEXT 4 PAGES, YOU WILL HAVE A NUMBER OF PLAYERS TO CHOOSE FROM - THE BETTER THE PLAYER, THE HIGHER THEIR COST! REMEMBER, YOU CAN T SPEND MORE THAN £100 MILLION! ONCE YOU HAVE CHOSEN A PLAYER, WRITE THEIR NAME ON THE TEAM SHEET BELOW!

....

....

....

....

COST: £   MILLION

13

MANAGER CHALLENGE

FIRST UP, PICK ONE GOALKEEPER. REMEMBER, YOU ONLY HAVE £100 MILLION TO SPEND ON YOUR WHOLE 11 MAN SQUAD! ONCE YOU HAVE CHOSEN, ADD THEIR NAME TO THE TEAMSHEET ON THE PREVIOUS PAGE!

GOALKEEPER	PRICE
MANUEL NEUER	£8 MILLION
ALISSON BECKER	£7 MILLION
GIGI DONNARUMMA	£7 MILLION
JAN OBLAK	£6 MILLION
DAVID DE GEA	£5 MILLION
HUGO LLORIS	£5 MILLION
EDOUARD MENDY	£4 MILLION
JORDAN PICKFORD	£3 MILLION

MANAGER CHALLENGE

NEXT, PICK THREE DEFENDERS. REMEMBER, YOU ONLY HAVE £100 MILLION TO SPEND ON YOUR WHOLE 11 MAN SQUAD! ONCE YOU HAVE CHOSEN, ADD THEIR NAMES TO THE TEAM SHEET!

DEFENDER	PRICE
VIRGIL VAN DIJK	£11 MILLION
SERGIO RAMOS	£10 MILLION
JOAO CANCELO	£8 MILLION
RAPHAEL VARANE	£7 MILLION
THIAGO SILVA	£7 MILLION
GIORGIO CHIELLINI	£6 MILLION
LUKE SHAW	£5 MILLION
HARRY MAGUIRE	£5 MILLION

MANAGER CHALLENGE

NEXT, PICK FOUR MIDFIELDERS. REMEMBER, YOU ONLY HAVE £100 MILLION TO SPEND ON YOUR WHOLE 11 MAN SQUAD! ONCE YOU HAVE CHOSEN, ADD THEIR NAMES TO THE TEAM SHEET!

MIDFIELDER	PRICE
KEVIN DE BRUYNE	£13 MILLION
N'GOLO KANTE	£11 MILLION
BRUNO FERNANDES	£10 MILLION
TONI KROOS	£9 MILLION
MARCO VERATTI	£8 MILLION
LUKA MODRIC	£8 MILLION
SERGIO BUSQUETS	£6 MILLION
MASON MOUNT	£6 MILLION

MANAGER CHALLENGE

FINALLY, PICK THREE FORWARDS. REMEMBER, YOU ONLY HAVE £100 MILLION TO SPEND ON YOUR WHOLE 11 MAN SQUAD! ONCE YOU HAVE CHOSEN, ADD THEIR NAMES TO THE TEAM SHEET!

FORWARD	PRICE
LIONEL MESSI	£15 MILLION
CRISTIANO RONALDO	£15 MILLION
KYLIAN MBAPPE	£12 MILLION
HARRY KANE	£11 MILLION
KARIM BENZEMA	£10 MILLION
SADIO MANE	£9 MILLION
HEUNG MIN SON	£8 MILLION
ROMELU LUKAKU	£7 MILLION

GOAL RECREATIONS #1

DRAW A LINE FROM THE BALL TO THE GOAL TO RECREATE THE EXACT PATH THE BALL TOOK IN THE FOLLOWING GOAL: ROBERTO CARLOS OUTSIDE OF THE BOOT FREE KICK VS FRANCE 1997

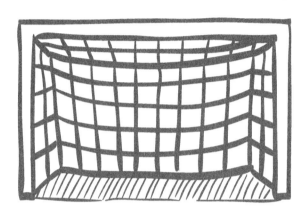

ANSWER ON PAGE 64!

TOP DEFENDERS: RATINGS

RATE SOME OF THE FOLLOWING FAMOUS WORLD CUP
DEFENDERS. ONCE YOU HAVE RATED EACH OF THEIR SKILLS,
TOTAL THEM UP TO SEE WHICH PLAYER YOU THINK IS BEST!

RAPHAEL VARANE

SPEED /10

TACKLING /10

HEADING /10

STRENGTH /10

PASSING /10

TOTAL /50

SERGIO RAMOS

SPEED /10

TACKLING /10

HEADING /10

STRENGTH /10

PASSING /10

TOTAL /50

THIAGO SILVA

SPEED /10

TACKLING /10

HEADING /10

STRENGTH /10

PASSING /10

TOTAL /50

TRENT ALEXANDER-ARNOLD

SPEED /10

TACKLING /10

HEADING /10

STRENGTH /10

PASSING /10

TOTAL /50

ORDER UP OPERATION

CAN YOU ORDER THE TOP 4 TEAMS IN THE 2014
WORLD CUP CORRECTLY, FROM 1ST PLACE TO 4TH?

GERMANY   NETHERLANDS

BRAZIL   ARGENTINA

1ST ....

2ND ....

3RD ....

4TH ....

ANSWERS ON PAGE 72!

WORLD CUP FACTS: HISTORY
TAKE A LOOK AT SOME OF THESE TOP FACTS
RELATING TO THE HISTORY OF THE WORLD CUP

⚽ THE FIRST EVER WORLD CUP WAS HELD IN 1930. URUGUAY HOSTED THE TOURNAMENT AND ALSO ENDED UP WINNING IT

⚽ THE FAMOUS WORLD CUP TROPHY HAS BEEN USED SINCE 1974

⚽ NOT ALL NATIONAL TEAMS FIRST ENTERED THE WORLD CUP. FOR EXAMPLE, ENGLAND S FIRST WORLD CUP WAS IN 1950

⚽ THE WORLD CUP HAS BEEN HELD EVERY FOUR YEARS SINCE IT STARTED, EXCEPT IN 1942 AND 1946 BECAUSE OF WORLD WAR II

TOP SQUAD: GERMANY 2014

TAKE A LOOK AT THIS FAMOUS WORLD CUP WINNING SQUAD.
GIVE IT A RATING ONCE YOU HAVE TAKEN A GOOD LOOK!

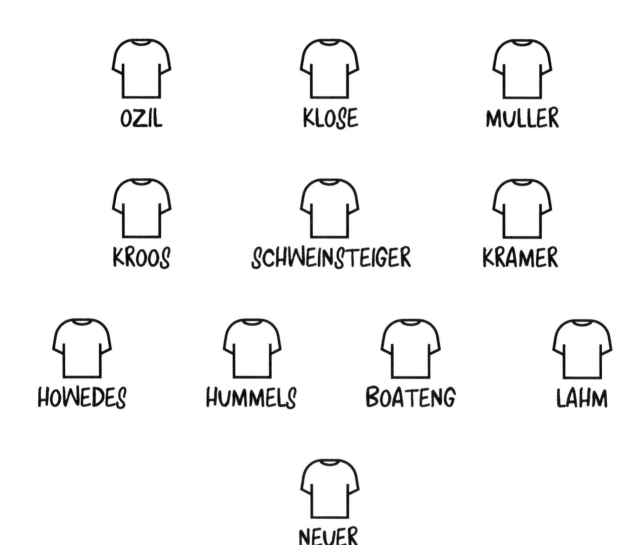

OZIL   KLOSE   MULLER

KROOS   SCHWEINSTEIGER   KRAMER

HOWEDES   HUMMELS   BOATENG   LAHM

NEUER

RATING: 8½ /10

MATCH UP MISSION

DRAW A LINE TO MATCH UP THE TEAM TO THE YEAR WHICH
THEY WON THE WORLD CUP

GERMANY   1966

ENGLAND   2010

FRANCE   2014

SPAIN   2018

ANSWERS ON PAGE 59!

ANAGRAMS: HOSTS

REARRANGE THE LETTERS TO WORK OUT WHAT FOOTBALL WORLD CUP HOST IS MADE UP OF THE SCRAMBLED WORD

AURISS = ...

ENTUID SSTTAE = ...

TRQAA = ...

OHUST FIACAR = ...

ANSWERS ON PAGE 82!

WHO AM I? #2

USE THE CLUES TO WORK OUT THE MYSTERY WORLD CUP PLAYER

1)   I WON THE WORLD CUP GOLDEN BALL FOR THE BEST PLAYER IN 2018

2)   MY NATIONAL TEAM'S HOME KIT COLOURS ARE USUALLY RED AND WHITE

3)   MY MAIN POSITION IS CENTRAL MIDFIELD

Luka Modrić

ANSWER ON PAGE 68!

ORDER UP OPERATION

CAN YOU ORDER THE TOP 4 TEAMS IN THE 1966 WORLD CUP CORRECTLY, FROM 1ST PLACE TO 4TH?

ENGLAND

SOVIET UNION (RUSSIA)

PORTUGAL

WEST GERMANY

1ST ....

2ND ....

3RD ....

4TH ....

ANSWERS ON PAGE 75!

QUIZ: PLAYERS

CAN YOU ANSWER ALL OF THE QUESTIONS BELOW CORRECTLY?

1) WHICH PLAYER CONTROVERSIALLY WINKED AT HIS TEAMS BENCH AFTER HELPING TO GET WAYNE ROONEY SENT OFF IN 2006?

2) WHO WAS THE TOP SCORER IN THE 2018 WORLD CUP?

3) WHICH PLAYER NICKNAMED 'THE EGYPTIAN KING PLAYED HIS FIRST WORLD CUP IN 2018?

4) WHICH PLAYER BIT ITALIAN DEFENDER CHIELLINI IN THE 2014 WORLD CUP?

5) HOW MANY WORLD CUP GOALS DID PELE SCORE?

ANSWERS ON PAGE 83!

WORLD CUP FACTS: FUN

TAKE A LOOK AT SOME OF THESE FUN FACTS ABOUT THE WORLD CUP

- ⚽ THE WORLD CUP IS THE MOST WATCHED FOOTBALL TOURNAMENT IN THE WORLD. IT IS ALSO GENERALLY CONSIDERED TO BE THE WORLD'S MOST POPULAR EVENT

- ⚽ NEARLY HALF THE WORLD'S POPULATION, 3.2 BILLION PEOPLE, WATCHED THE 2014 WORLD CUP

- ⚽ THE WORLD CUP TROPHY WAS STOLEN BEFORE THE 1966 WORLD CUP. AFTER BEING MISSING FOR 7 DAYS, IT WAS FOUND BY A DOG CALLED PICKLES!

- ⚽ IN THE 2026 WORLD CUP, THE NUMBER OF TEAMS WHO QUALIFY AND PLAY IN THE FINAL STAGES WILL INCREASE FROM 32 TO 48

WORD SEARCH: TOP TEAMS

CAN YOU FIND ALL THE TOP WORLD CUP TEAMS IN THE WORD SEARCH?

```
C E L C A R G E N T I N A K I
A I H E W O O D S P O Z A C T
R P O R T U G A L S G Y C E A
V W T A P E Q J N W A E K X L
E A C S G E L O B T E N S P Y
F T N E A B O Y K I N O O T R
R I V N A C G T N N G I N C E
A C I O K B E I O T L E P R K
N J O H F Y R S S P A I N N E
C Y G W J Y M A E W N P V E N
E W X H U I A B Z O D E H E N
V J O O V Z N C O I B A Q N A
U R U G U A Y E O I L P V E B
```

ITALY   PORTUGAL   SPAIN
URUGUAY   BRAZIL   ARGENTINA
GERMANY   ENGLAND   FRANCE

ANSWERS ON PAGE 88!

FOOTBALL DESIGN

HAVE A GO AT DESIGNING YOUR ULTIMATE WORLD CUP FOOTBALL!

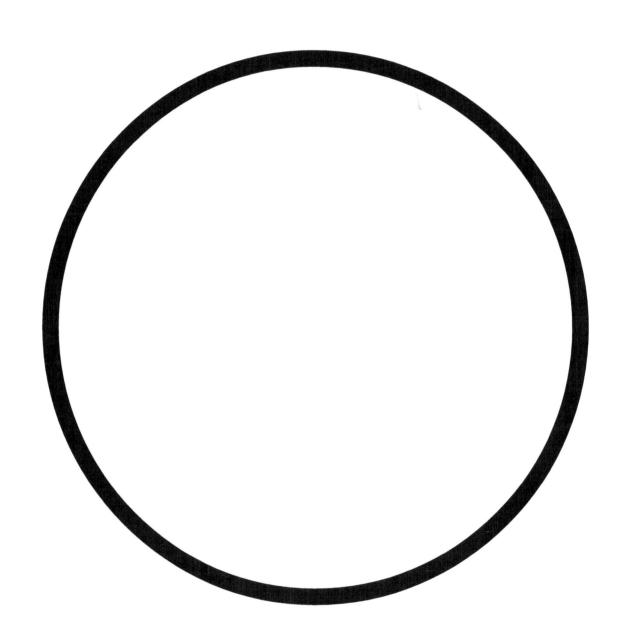

TOP MIDFIELDERS: RATINGS

RATE SOME OF THE FOLLOWING FAMOUS WORLD CUP MIDFIELDERS. ONCE YOU HAVE RATED EACH OF THEIR SKILLS, TOTAL THEM UP TO SEE WHICH PLAYER YOU THINK IS BEST!

KEVIN DE BRUYNE

SPEED	7/10
SHOOTING	8/10
PASSING	10/10
TACKLING	7/10
DRIBBLING	8/10
TOTAL	40/50

LUKA MODRIC

SPEED	8/10
SHOOTING	9/10
PASSING	6/10
TACKLING	7/10
DRIBBLING	7/10
TOTAL	4/50

PAUL POGBA

SPEED	7/10
SHOOTING	9/10
PASSING	7/10
TACKLING	8/10
DRIBBLING	7/10
TOTAL	38/50

TONI KROOS

SPEED	8/10
SHOOTING	7/10
PASSING	9/10
TACKLING	8/10
DRIBBLING	8/10
TOTAL	4/50

TOP SQUAD: SPAIN 2010

TAKE A LOOK AT THIS FAMOUS WORLD CUP WINNING SQUAD.
GIVE IT A RATING ONCE YOU HAVE TAKEN A GOOD LOOK!

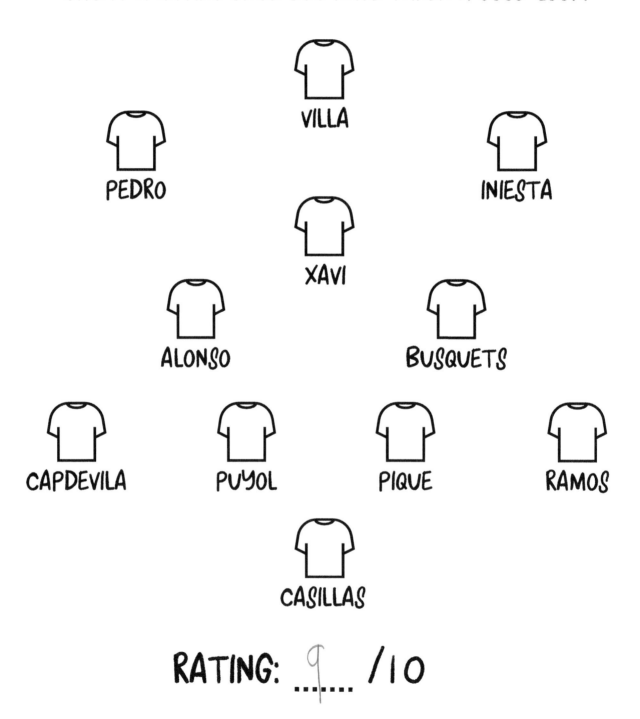

RATING: ...9.... /10

ORDER UP OPERATION

CAN YOU ORDER THE TOP 4 TEAMS IN THE 2006 WORLD CUP CORRECTLY, FROM 1ST PLACE TO 4TH?

GERMANY

FRANCE

ITALY

PORTUGAL

1ST *Italy*

2ND *France*

3RD *Germany*

4TH *Portougal*

ANSWERS ON PAGE 74!

GOAL RECREATIONS #2

DRAW A LINE FROM THE BALL TO THE GOAL TO RECREATE THE
EXACT PATH THE BALL TOOK IN THE FOLLOWING GOAL:
CRISTIANO RONALDO FREE KICK VS SPAIN 2018

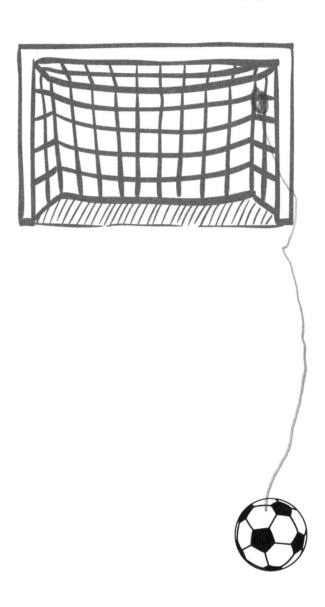

ANSWER ON PAGE 65!

QUIZ: GENERAL

CAN YOU ANSWER ALL OF THE QUESTIONS BELOW CORRECTLY?

1) WHAT COMPANY MADE THE BALL FOR THE 2018 WORLD CUP? *Adidas*

2) HOW OFTEN IS THE WORLD CUP HELD? *4 years*

3) HOW MANY TEAMS USUALLY QUALIFY FOR THE WORLD CUP? *32*

4) WHAT WOULD HAPPEN IN A FINAL IF BOTH TEAMS ARE STILL DRAWING AFTER 90 MINUTES AND EXTRA TIME? *penalties*

5) WHAT WAS THE DOG CALLED THAT FOUND THE TROPHY BEFORE THE 1966 WORLD CUP?

ANSWERS ON PAGE 86!

ANAGRAMS: TEAMS

REARRANGE THE LETTERS TO WORK OUT WHAT TEAM IS MADE UP OF THE SCRAMBLED WORD

AGANH   = ...

CEEGER   = ...

GELBUIM   = ...

OTSUH KEROA   = ...

ANSWERS ON PAGE 79!

WHO AM I? #3

USE THE CLUES TO WORK OUT THE MYSTERY WORLD CUP PLAYER

1)   I WON THE YOUNG PLAYER AWARD AT THE 2018 WORLD CUP

2)   I BEGAN MY PROFESSIONAL SENIOR CAREER AT MONACO

3)   I AM ONE OF THE FASTEST FOOTBALLERS

....

ANSWER ON PAGE 69!

MATCH UP MISSION

DRAW A LINE TO MATCH UP THE YEAR TO THE PLACE WHERE
THE WORLD CUP WAS, OR WILL BE, HOSTED

2022   BRAZIL

2018   ENGLAND

2014   QATAR

1966   RUSSIA

ANSWERS ON PAGE 58!

WORLD CUP FACTS: CAPS

TAKE A LOOK AT THE HIGHEST CAPPED PLAYERS OF THE PAST IN WORLD CUP TOURNAMENTS. THESE PLAYERS HAVE ALL NOW RETIRED

PLAYER	CAPS
LOTHAR MATTHAUS (GERMANY)	25
MIROSLAV KLOSE (GERMANY)	24
PAOLO MALDINI (ITALY)	23
DIEGO MARADONA (ARGENTINA)	21
UWE SEELER (GERMANY)	21
WLADYSLAW ZMUDA (POLAND)	21
CAFU (BRAZIL)	20
PHILIP LAHM (GERMANY)	20
GRZEGORZ LATO (POLAND)	20
JAVIER MASCHERANO (ARGENTINA)	20

BOOT DESIGN

HAVE A GO AT DESIGNING YOUR ULTIMATE WORLD CUP FOOTBALL BOOT!

ORDER UP OPERATION

CAN YOU ORDER THE TOP 4 TEAMS IN THE 2018 WORLD CUP CORRECTLY, FROM 1ST PLACE TO 4TH?

BELGIUM

ENGLAND

FRANCE

CROATIA

1ST ....

2ND ....

3RD ....

4TH ....

ANSWERS ON PAGE 71!

TOP SQUAD: ITALY 2006

TAKE A LOOK AT THIS FAMOUS WORLD CUP WINNING SQUAD.
GIVE IT A RATING ONCE YOU HAVE TAKEN A GOOD LOOK!

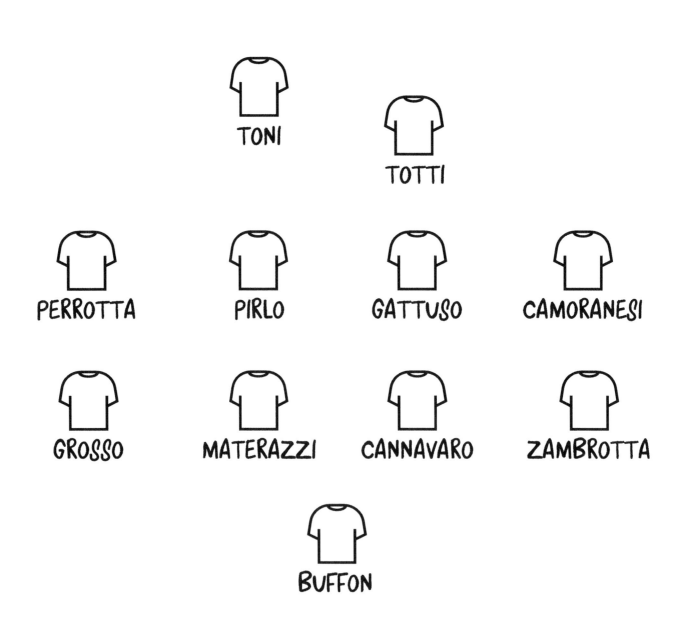

RATING: .... /10

TOP FORWARDS: RATINGS

RATE SOME OF THE FOLLOWING FAMOUS WORLD CUP FORWARDS. ONCE YOU HAVE RATED EACH OF THEIR SKILLS, TOTAL THEM UP TO SEE WHICH PLAYER YOU THINK IS BEST!

CRISTIANO RONALDO

SPEED	/10
SHOOTING	/10
HEADING	/10
STRENGTH	/10
DRIBBLING	/10
TOTAL	/50

HARRY KANE

SPEED	/10
SHOOTING	/10
HEADING	/10
STRENGTH	/10
DRIBBLING	/10
TOTAL	/50

LIONEL MESSI

SPEED	/10
SHOOTING	/10
HEADING	/10
STRENGTH	/10
DRIBBLING	/10
TOTAL	/50

NEYMAR

SPEED	/10
SHOOTING	/10
HEADING	/10
STRENGTH	/10
DRIBBLING	/10
TOTAL	/50

WORLD CUP FACTS: FORMAT

TAKE A LOOK AT SOME OF THESE KEY FACTS ABOUT HOW THE WORLD CUP RUNS AND OPERATES

- ⚽ THE WORLD CUP IS HELD ONCE EVERY FOUR YEARS

- ⚽ QUALIFICATION MATCHES TAKE PLACE PRIOR TO THE WORLD CUP IN ORDER TO ESTABLISH THE FINAL 32 TEAMS WHO WILL PLAY IN THE WORLD CUP. THE HOST AUTOMATICALLY QUALIFIES

- ⚽ THE FINAL 32 TEAMS PLAY IN 8 RANDOMLY SELECTED GROUPS OF 4 TEAMS. THE TOP 2 TEAMS IN EACH GROUP GO TO THE NEXT STAGE

- ⚽ THE KNOCKOUT STAGE IS NEXT. TEAMS PLAY EACH OTHER ONCE, THE LOSER GETTING KNOCKED OUT OF THE TOURNAMENT AND THE WINNER ADVANCING TO THE NEXT KNOCKOUT MATCH. THIS GOES ON UNTIL TWO TEAMS ARE LEFT, WHO PLAY TO WIN IN THE FINAL

WORD SEARCH: TOP PLAYERS

CAN YOU FIND ALL THE TOP WORLD CUP PLAYERS IN THE WORD SEARCH?

```
C M E S S I N G P E K L A W X
H T A B M I L E S E E R W D J
T E M O D R I C C P L A C P B
S M C Y Y O R C C Q R E U M K
C E L C I B R G Q L I E J K L
A A H E W B O D S T O A A C O
R G O O F E I A S S R Y C E S
V Z I D A N E J N W O E K X E
E A C S G E L O B T N R S P A
R L N E A B O Y K I A O O T R
M A R A D O N A N N L I N C E
A C I O K M A I O T D E P R K
X J O J F Y I S O J O K A N E
```

KLOSE	ROBBEN	RONALDO
ZIDANE	MARADONA	PELE
KANE	MODRIC	MESSI

ANSWERS ON PAGE 87!

GOAL RECREATIONS #3

DRAW A LINE FROM THE BALL TO THE GOAL TO RECREATE THE
EXACT PATH THE BALL TOOK IN THE FOLLOWING GOAL:
GRIEZMANN'S PENALTY IN THE 2018 WORLD CUP FINAL VS CROATIA

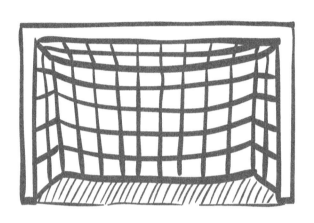

ANSWER ON PAGE 66!

MATCH UP MISSION

DRAW A LINE TO MATCH UP THE WORLD CUP LEGEND WITH THEIR NATIONAL TEAM

PELE   BRAZIL

BOBBY CHARLTON   ARGENTINA

ZINEDINE ZIDANE   ENGLAND

DIEGO MARADONA   FRANCE

ANSWERS ON PAGE 60!

QUIZ: SCORES

CAN YOU ANSWER ALL OF THE QUESTIONS BELOW CORRECTLY?

1) WHAT TWO TEAMS PLAYED IN THE WORLD CUP 2018 FINAL + WHAT WAS THE SCORE?

   France 4 - 2 Croatia

2) WHAT WAS THE SCORE BETWEEN SWEDEN VS ENGLAND IN THE 2018 QUARTER FINAL?

3) WHAT WAS THE SCORE BETWEEN NETHERLANDS VS SPAIN IN THE 2010 FINAL?

   Spain 1 - 0 Netherlands

4) WHAT WAS THE SCORE BETWEEN BELGIUM VS ENGLAND IN THE 2018 3RD PLACE PLAY OFF?

5) WHAT TWO TEAMS PLAYED IN THE 2014 WORLD CUP FINAL + WHAT WAS THE SCORE?

   Germany 1 - 0 Argentina

ANSWERS ON PAGE 85!

WHO AM I? #4

USE THE CLUES TO WORK OUT THE MYSTERY WORLD CUP PLAYER

1) I PLAYED IN THE SAME SQUAD AS PIRLO AND TOTTI WHEN I WON THE WORLD CUP

2) I USED TO CAPTAIN MY NATIONAL TEAM

3) I HAVE NEVER SCORED A GOAL FOR MY TEAM

....

ANSWER ON PAGE 70!

WORLD CUP FACTS: PAST SCORERS

TAKE A LOOK AT THE HIGHEST TOP SCORERS OF THE PAST IN WORLD CUP TOURNAMENTS. THESE PLAYERS HAVE ALL NOW RETIRED

PLAYER	GOALS
MIROSLAV KLOSE (GERMANY)	16
RONALDO (BRAZIL)	15
GERD MULLER (WEST GERMANY)	14
JUST FONTAINE (FRANCE)	13
PELE (BRAZIL)	12
SANDOR KOCSIS (HUNGARY)	11
JURGEN KLINSMANN (GERMANY)	11
HELMUT RAHN (WEST GERMANY)	10
GARY LINEKAR (ENGLAND)	10
GABRIEL BATISTUTA (ARGENTINA)	10

ORDER UP OPERATION

CAN YOU ORDER THESE WORLD CUP STADIUMS FROM
HIGHEST TO LOWEST IN TERMS OF CAPACITY?
1ST = LARGEST CAPACITY, 4TH = SMALLEST CAPACITY

CAMP NOU   OLYMPIASTADION

WEMBLEY   SAN SIRO

1ST ....

2ND ....

3RD ....

4TH ....

ANSWERS ON PAGE 78!

ANAGRAMS: BRANDS

REARRANGE THE LETTERS TO WORK OUT WHAT FOOTBALL WORLD CUP BRAND IS MADE UP OF THE SCRAMBLED WORD

EWN ALCBEAN = ...

ENKI = ...

UMPA = ...

DDAASI = ...

ANSWERS ON PAGE 81!

TOP GOALKEEPERS: RATINGS

RATE SOME OF THE FOLLOWING FAMOUS WORLD CUP GOALKEEPERS. ONCE YOU HAVE RATED EACH OF THEIR SKILLS, TOTAL THEM UP TO SEE WHICH PLAYER YOU THINK IS BEST!

DAVID DE GEA

SPEED	/10
REACTIONS	/10
DIVING	/10
CATCHING	/10
KICKING	/10
TOTAL	/50

HUGO LLORIS

SPEED	/10
REACTIONS	/10
DIVING	/10
CATCHING	/10
KICKING	/10
TOTAL	/50

MANUEL NEUER

SPEED	/10
REACTIONS	/10
DIVING	/10
CATCHING	/10
KICKING	/10
TOTAL	/50

THIBAUT COURTOIS

SPEED	/10
REACTIONS	/10
DIVING	/10
CATCHING	/10
KICKING	/10
TOTAL	/50

MATCH UP MISSION

DRAW A LINE TO MATCH UP THE FAMOUS WORLD CUP PLAYER
TO THEIR USUAL PLAYING POSITION

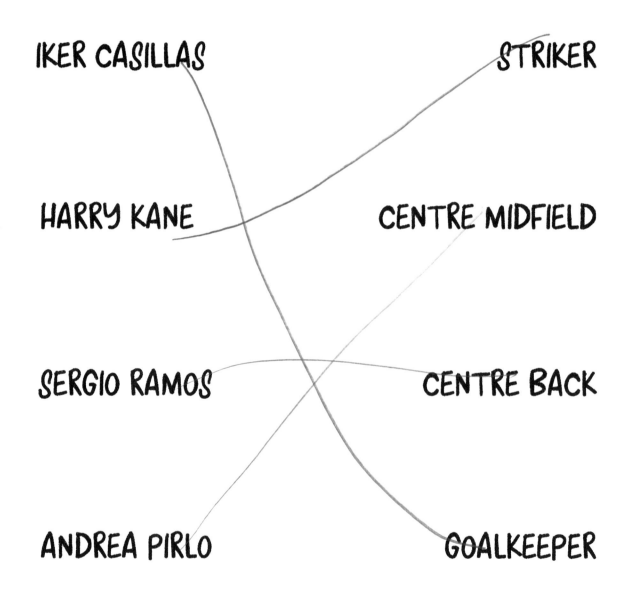

IKER CASILLAS

STRIKER

HARRY KANE

CENTRE MIDFIELD

SERGIO RAMOS

CENTRE BACK

ANDREA PIRLO

GOALKEEPER

ANSWERS ON PAGE 63!

TOP SQUAD: BRAZIL 2002

TAKE A LOOK AT THIS FAMOUS WORLD CUP WINNING SQUAD.
GIVE IT A RATING ONCE YOU HAVE TAKEN A GOOD LOOK!

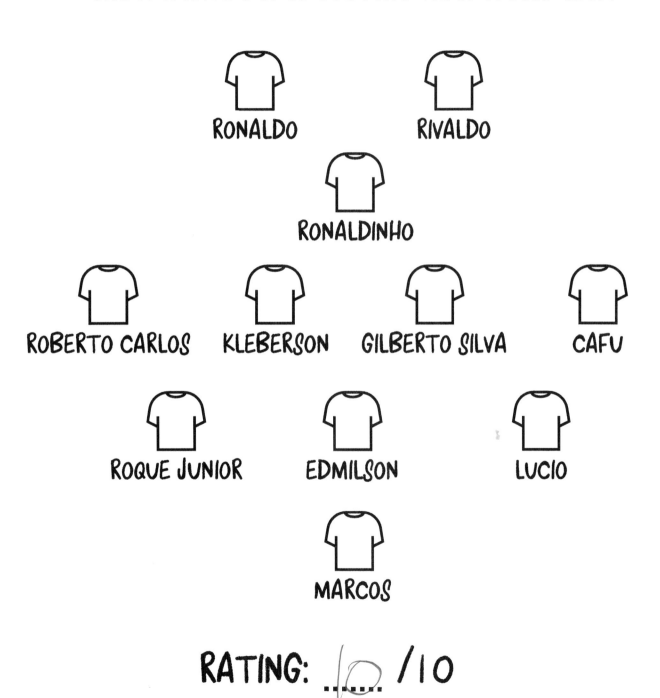

RATING: 10 /10

ORDER UP OPERATION

CAN YOU ORDER THE TOP 4 TEAMS IN THE 2010 WORLD CUP CORRECTLY, FROM 1ST PLACE TO 4TH?

NETHERLANDS   URUGUAY

GERMANY   SPAIN

1ST ....

2ND ....

3RD ....

4TH ....

ANSWERS ON PAGE 78!

ANSWERS

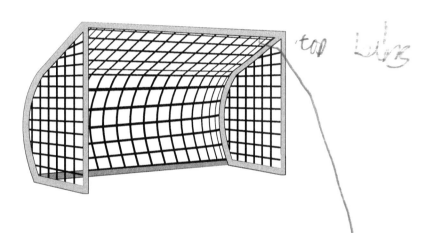

DID YOU MISS THE TARGET?

MATCH UP MISSION

DRAW A LINE TO MATCH UP THE YEAR TO THE PLACE WHERE THE WORLD CUP WAS, OR WILL BE, HOSTED

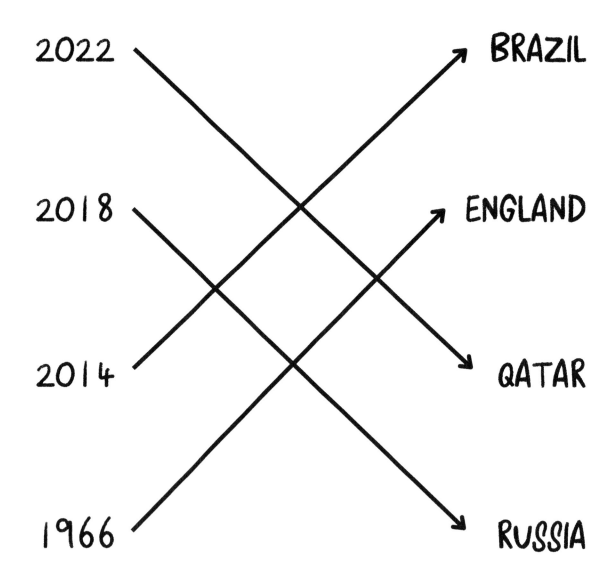

2022

2018

2014

1966

BRAZIL

ENGLAND

QATAR

RUSSIA

MATCH UP MISSION

DRAW A LINE TO MATCH UP THE TEAM TO THE YEAR WHICH
THEY WON THE WORLD CUP

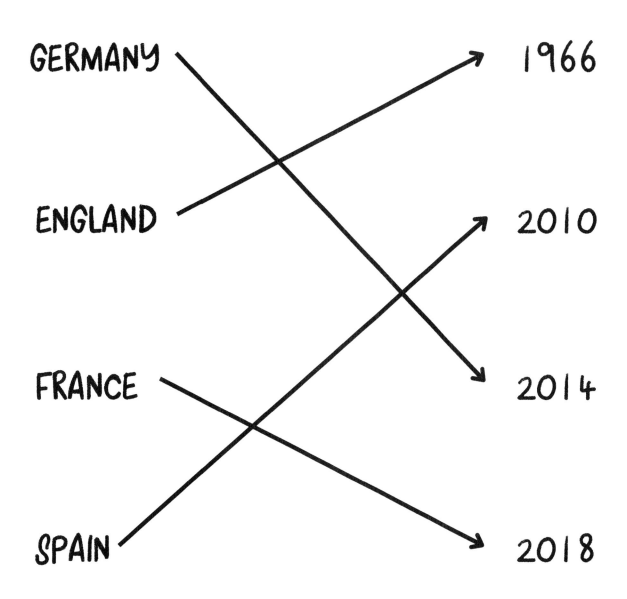

GERMANY — 1966

ENGLAND — 2010

FRANCE — 2014

SPAIN — 2018

ANSWERS ON PAGE X!

MATCH UP MISSION

DRAW A LINE TO MATCH UP THE WORLD CUP LEGEND WITH THEIR NATIONAL TEAM

PELE →→→→→→→ BRAZIL

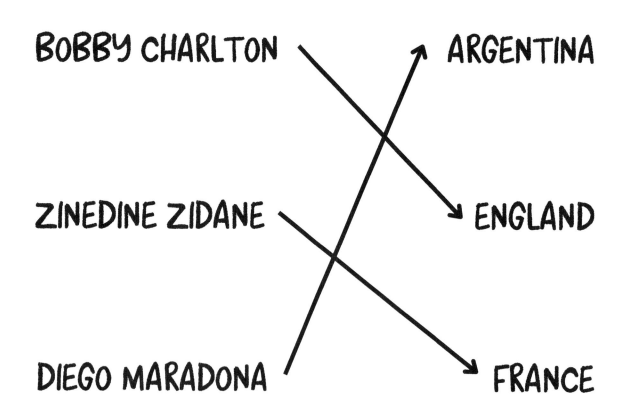

BOBBY CHARLTON   ARGENTINA

ZINEDINE ZIDANE   ENGLAND

DIEGO MARADONA   FRANCE

ANSWERS ON PAGE X!

MATCH UP MISSION

DRAW A LINE TO MATCH UP THE TEAM TO THEIR USUAL HOME KIT COLOURS

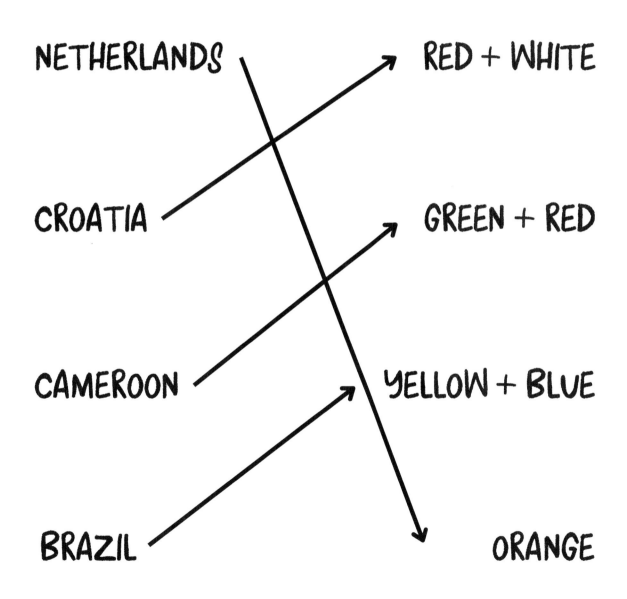

NETHERLANDS

CROATIA

CAMEROON

BRAZIL

RED + WHITE

GREEN + RED

YELLOW + BLUE

ORANGE

MATCH UP MISSION

DRAW A LINE TO MATCH UP THE WORLD CUP STADIUM TO ITS LOCATION

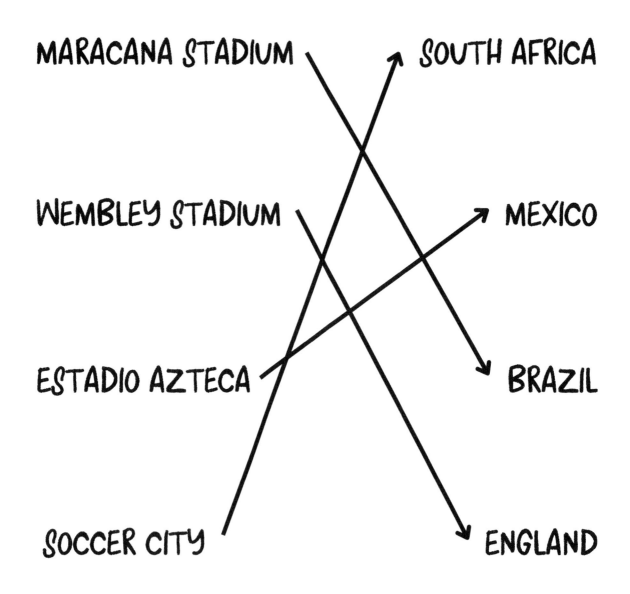

MARACANA STADIUM

WEMBLEY STADIUM

ESTADIO AZTECA

SOCCER CITY

SOUTH AFRICA

MEXICO

BRAZIL

ENGLAND

MATCH UP MISSION

DRAW A LINE TO MATCH UP THE FAMOUS WORLD CUP PLAYER
TO THEIR USUAL PLAYING POSITION

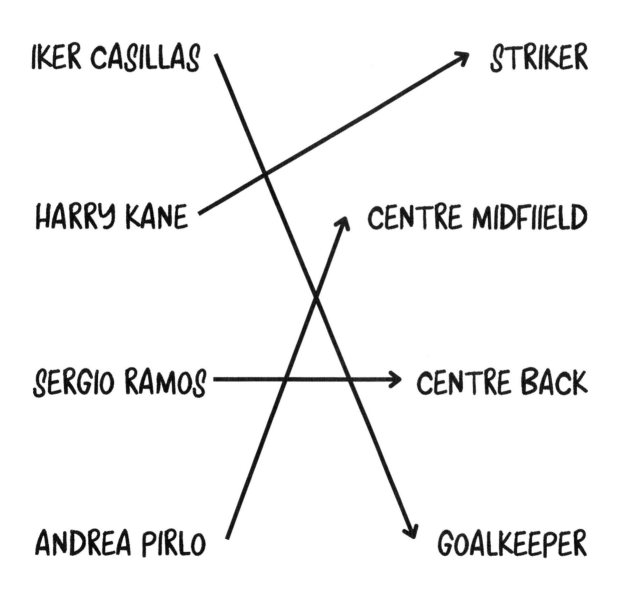

IKER CASILLAS

HARRY KANE

SERGIO RAMOS

ANDREA PIRLO

STRIKER

CENTRE MIDFIIELD

CENTRE BACK

GOALKEEPER

GOAL RECREATIONS #1

DRAW A LINE FROM THE BALL TO THE GOAL TO RECREATE THE EXACT PATH THE BALL TOOK IN THE FOLLOWING GOAL: ROBERTO CARLOS OUTSIDE OF THE BOOT FREE KICK VS FRANCE 1997

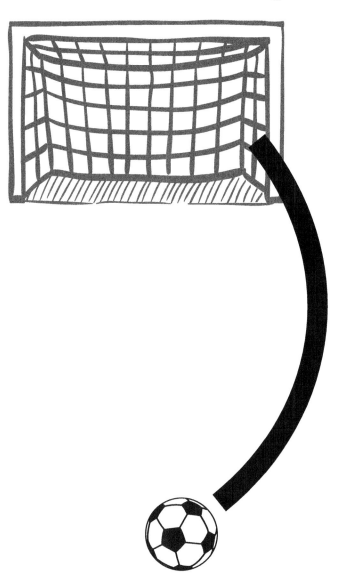

GOAL RECREATIONS #2

DRAW A LINE FROM THE BALL TO THE GOAL TO RECREATE THE
EXACT PATH THE BALL TOOK IN THE FOLLOWING GOAL:
CRISTIANO RONALDO FREE KICK VS SPAIN 2018

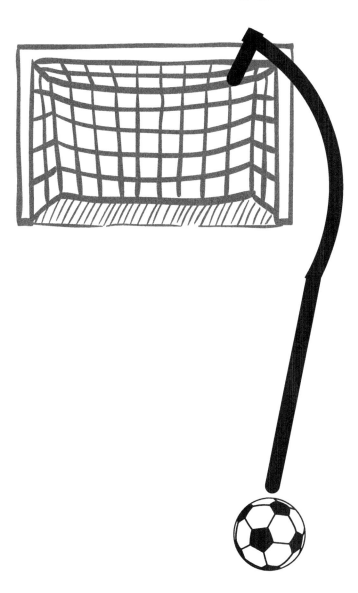

GOAL RECREATIONS #3

DRAW A LINE FROM THE BALL TO THE GOAL TO RECREATE THE EXACT PATH THE BALL TOOK IN THE FOLLOWING GOAL: GRIEZMANN'S PENALTY IN THE 2018 WORLD CUP FINAL VS CROATIA

WHO AM I? #1

USE THE CLUES TO WORK OUT THE MYSTERY WORLD CUP PLAYER

1) I CAPTAINED MY NATIONAL TEAM

2) I USUALLY WORE THE NUMBER 7 SHIRT

3) I INSPIRED THE FILM 'BEND IT LIKE ...'

DAVID BECKHAM

WHO AM I? #2

1)   I WON THE WORLD CUP GOLDEN BALL FOR THE BEST PLAYER IN 2018

2)   MY NATIONAL TEAM'S HOME KIT COLOURS ARE USUALLY RED AND WHITE

3)   MY MAIN POSITION IS CENTRAL MIDFIELD

LUKA MODRIC
....

WHO AM I? #3

USE THE CLUES TO WORK OUT THE MYSTERY WORLD CUP PLAYER

1) I WON THE YOUNG PLAYER AWARD AT THE 2018 WORLD CUP

2) I BEGAN MY PROFESSIONAL SENIOR CAREER AT MONACO

3) I AM ONE OF THE FASTEST FOOTBALLERS

KYLIAN MBAPPE
....

WHO AM I? #4

USE THE CLUES TO WORK OUT THE MYSTERY WORLD CUP PLAYER

1) I PLAYED IN THE SAME SQUAD AS PIRLO AND TOTTI WHEN I WON THE WORLD CUP

2) I USED TO CAPTAIN MY NATIONAL TEAM

3) I HAVE NEVER SCORED A GOAL FOR MY TEAM

GIANLUIGI BUFFON
....

ORDER UP OPERATION

CAN YOU ORDER THE TOP 4 TEAMS IN THE 2018 WORLD CUP CORRECTLY, FROM 1ST PLACE TO 4TH?

BELGIUM

ENGLAND

FRANCE

CROATIA

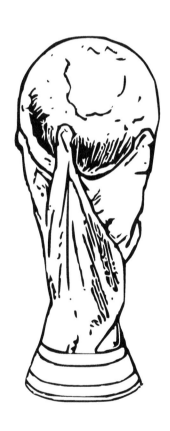

1ST ....FRANCE.................................

2ND ....CROATIA...............................

3RD ....BELGIUM..............................

4TH ....ENGLAND.............................

ORDER UP OPERATION

CAN YOU ORDER THE TOP 4 TEAMS IN THE 2014 WORLD CUP CORRECTLY, FROM 1ST PLACE TO 4TH?

GERMANY   NETHERLANDS

BRAZIL   ARGENTINA

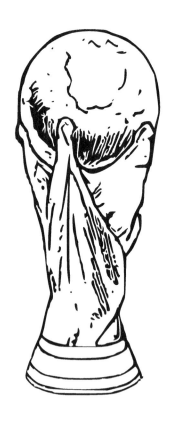

1ST **GERMANY**

2ND **ARGENTINA**

3RD **NETHERLANDS**

4TH **BRAZIL**

ORDER UP OPERATION

CAN YOU ORDER THE TOP 4 TEAMS IN THE 2010 WORLD CUP CORRECTLY, FROM 1ST PLACE TO 4TH?

NETHERLANDS   URUGUAY

GERMANY   SPAIN

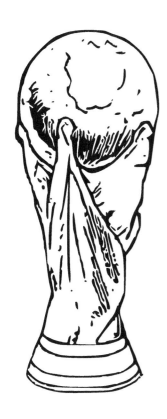

1ST ...... SPAIN ....

2ND ...... NETHERLANDS ......

3RD ...... GERMANY ....

4TH ...... URUGUAY ....

ORDER UP OPERATION

CAN YOU ORDER THE TOP 4 TEAMS IN THE 2006 WORLD CUP CORRECTLY, FROM 1ST PLACE TO 4TH?

GERMANY

FRANCE

ITALY

PORTUGAL

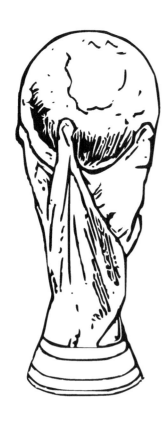

1ST .... ITALY ....

2ND .... FRANCE ....

3RD .... GERMANY ....

4TH .... PORTUGAL ....

ORDER UP OPERATION

CAN YOU ORDER THE TOP 4 TEAMS IN THE 1966 WORLD CUP CORRECTLY, FROM 1ST PLACE TO 4TH?

ENGLAND   SOVIET UNION (RUSSIA)

PORTUGAL   WEST GERMANY

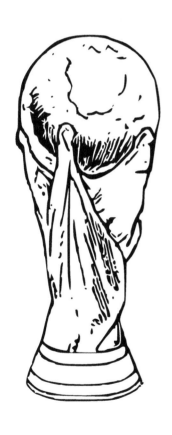

1ST ENGLAND

2ND WEST GERMANY

3RD PORTUGAL

4TH SOVIET UNION (RUSSIA)

ORDER UP OPERATION

CAN YOU ORDER THESE PAST PLAYERS FROM HIGHEST
TO LOWEST IN TERMS OF WORLD CUP CAPS?
1ST = MOST CAPS, 4TH = LEAST CAPS

LAHM   THIERY HENRY

GERRARD   PELE

1ST LAHM (20)

2ND THIERY HENRY (17)

3RD PELE (14)

4TH GERRARD (12)

ORDER UP OPERATION

CAN YOU ORDER THESE PAST PLAYERS FROM HIGHEST TO LOWEST IN TERMS OF WORLD CUP GOALS?
1ST = MOST GOALS, 4TH = LEAST GOALS

KLOSE   ROONEY

MARADONA   ROBBEN

1ST KLOSE (16)

2ND MARADONA (8)

3RD ROBBEN (6)

4TH ROONEY (*1)

ORDER UP OPERATION

CAN YOU ORDER THESE WORLD CUP STADIUMS FROM HIGHEST TO LOWEST IN TERMS OF CAPACITY?
1ST = LARGEST CAPACITY, 4TH = SMALLEST CAPACITY

CAMP NOU   OLYMPIASTADION

WEMBLEY   SAN SIRO

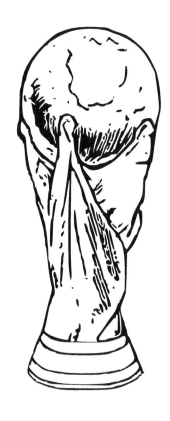

1ST CAMP NOU (99,354)

2ND WEMBLEY (90,000)

3RD SAN SIRO (80,018)

4TH OLYMPIASTADION (74,475)

ANAGRAMS: TEAMS

REARRANGE THE LETTERS TO WORK OUT WHAT
TEAM IS MADE UP OF THE SCRAMBLED WORD

AGANH = GHANA

CEEGER = GREECE

GELBUIM = BELGIUM

OTSUH KEROA = SOUTH KOREA

ANAGRAMS: PLAYERS

REARRANGE THE LETTERS TO WORK OUT WHAT
PLAYER IS MADE UP OF THE SCRAMBLED WORD

RZAHDA = HAZARD

EABL = BALE

LARAPMD = LAMPARD

LUPOY = PUYOL

ANAGRAMS: BRANDS

REARRANGE THE LETTERS TO WORK OUT WHAT FOOTBALL WORLD CUP BRAND IS MADE UP OF THE SCRAMBLED WORD

EWN ALCBEAN   =   NEW BALANCE

ENKI   =   NIKE

UMPA   =   PUMA

DDAASI   =   ADIDAS

ANAGRAMS: HOSTS

REARRANGE THE LETTERS TO WORK OUT WHAT FOOTBALL WORLD CUP HOST IS MADE UP OF THE SCRAMBLED WORD

AURISS = RUSSIA

ENTUID SSTTAE = UNITED STATES

TRQAA = QATAR

OHUST FIACAR = SOUTH AFRICA

QUIZ: PLAYERS

CAN YOU ANSWER ALL OF THE QUESTIONS BELOW CORRECTLY?

1) WHICH PLAYER CONTROVERSIALLY WINKED AT HIS TEAMS BENCH AFTER HELPING TO GET WAYNE ROONEY SENT OFF IN 2006?

CRISTIANO RONALDO

2) WHO WAS THE TOP SCORER IN THE 2018 WORLD CUP?

HARRY KANE

3) WHICH PLAYER NICKNAMED 'THE EGYPTIAN KING' PLAYED HIS FIRST WORLD CUP IN 2018?

MO SALAH

4) WHICH PLAYER BIT ITALIAN DEFENDER CHIELLINI IN THE 2014 WORLD CUP?

LUIZ SUAREZ

5) HOW MANY WORLD CUP GOALS DID PELE SCORE?

12

QUIZ: TEAMS

CAN YOU ANSWER ALL OF THE QUESTIONS BELOW CORRECTLY?

1) WHICH TEAM WON THE FIRST EVER WORLD CUP?

URUGUAY

2) HOW MANY TIME HAVE URUGUAY WON THE WORLD CUP?

TWICE

3) WHAT TEAM IS NICKNAMED 'THE THREE LIONS'?

ENGLAND

4) WHAT ARE THE USUAL COLOURS OF AREGNTINA'S HOME JERSEY?

BLUE + WHITE

5) WHAT YEAR DID ENGLAND FIRST HOST THE WORLD CUP?

1966

QUIZ: SCORES

CAN YOU ANSWER ALL OF THE QUESTIONS BELOW CORRECTLY?

1) WHAT TWO TEAMS PLAYED IN THE WORLD CUP 2018 FINAL + WHAT WAS THE SCORE?

   FRANCE 4 - 2 CROATIA

2) WHAT WAS THE SCORE BETWEEN SWEDEN VS ENGLAND IN THE 2018 QUARTER FINAL?

   SWEDEN 0 - 2 ENGLAND

3) WHAT WAS THE SCORE BETWEEN NETHERLANDS VS SPAIN IN THE 2010 FINAL?

   NETHERLANDS 0 - 1 SPAIN

4) WHAT WAS THE SCORE BETWEEN BELGIUM VS ENGLAND IN THE 2018 3RD PLACE PLAY OFF?

   BELGIUM 2 - 0 ENGLAND

5) WHAT TWO TEAMS PLAYED IN THE 2014 WORLD CUP FINAL + WHAT WAS THE SCORE?

   GERMANY 1 - 0 ARGENTINA

QUIZ: GENERAL

CAN YOU ANSWER ALL OF THE QUESTIONS BELOW CORRECTLY?

1) WHAT COMPANY MADE THE BALL FOR THE 2018 WORLD CUP?

   ADIDAS

2) HOW OFTEN IS THE WORLD CUP HELD?

   EVERY 4 YEARS

3) HOW MANY TEAMS USUALLY QUALIFY FOR THE WORLD CUP?

   32

4) WHAT WOULD HAPPEN IN A FINAL IF BOTH TEAMS ARE STILL DRAWING AFTER 90 MINUTES AND EXTRA TIME?

   PENALTIES

5) WHAT WAS THE DOG CALLED THAT FOUND THE TROPHY BEFORE THE 1966 WORLD CUP?

   PICKLES

WORD SEARCH: TOP PLAYERS

CAN YOU FIND ALL THE TOP WORLD CUP PLAYERS IN THE WORD SEARCH?

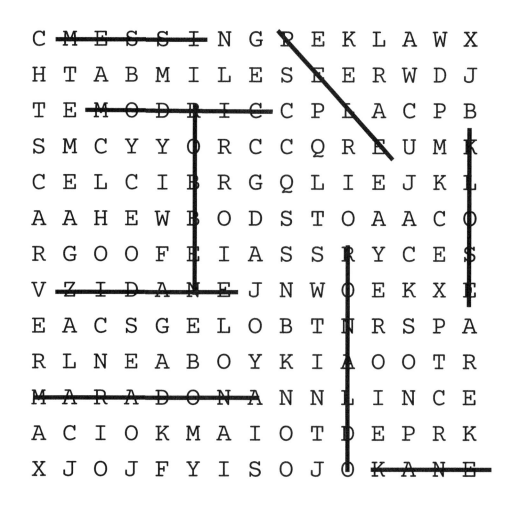

```
C M E S S I N G R E K L A W X
H T A B M I L E S E E R W D J
T E M O D R I C C P L A C P B
S M C Y Y O R C C Q R E U M K
C E L C I B R G Q L I E J K L
A A H E W B O D S T O A A C O
R G O O F E I A S S R Y C E S
V Z I D A N E J N W O E K X E
E A C S G E L O B T N R S P A
R L N E A B O Y K I A O O T R
M A R A D O N A N N L I N C E
A C I O K M A I O T D E P R K
X J O J F Y I S O J O K A N E
```

KLOSE   ROBBEN   RONALDO

ZIDANE   MARADONA   PELE

KANE   MODRIC   MESSI

WORD SEARCH: TOP TEAMS

CAN YOU FIND ALL THE TOP WORLD CUP TEAMS IN THE WORD SEARCH?

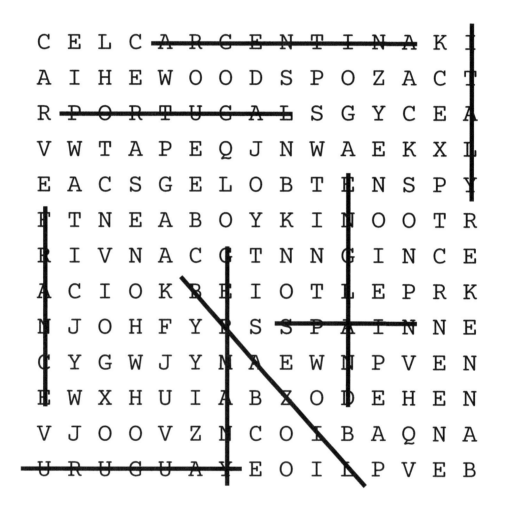

ITALY   PORTUGAL   SPAIN

URUGUAY   BRAZIL   ARGENTINA

GERMANY   ENGLAND   FRANCE

WORD SEARCH: TOP MANAGERS

CAN YOU FIND ALL THE WORLD CUP MANAGERS IN THE WORD SEARCH?

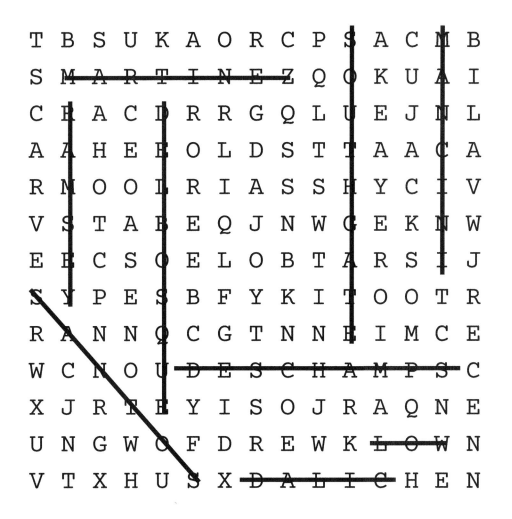

T B S U K A O R C P S A C M B
S M A R T I N E Z Q O K U A I
C R A C D R R G Q L U E J N L
A A H E O L D S T T A A C A
R M O O R I A S S H Y C I V
V S T A B E Q J N W G E K N W
E E C S O E L O B T A R S I J
S Y P E S B F Y K I T O O T R
R A N N Q C G T N N E I M C E
W C N O U D E S C H A M P S C
X J R I E Y I S O J R A Q N E
U N G W O F D R E W K L O W N
V T X H U S X D A L I C H E N

DESCHAMPS	MANCINI	RAMSEY
DEL BOSQUE	MARTINEZ	LOW
SOUTHGATE	SANTOS	DALIC

Printed in Great Britain
by Amazon

10922928R00052